EMILIE PARIET TODD HELM

Abraham Lincoln's "Little Sister"

First Edition

By
Dorothy Darnall Jones

Formatted by: Ron Harsin

Deer Trail Publishing
Lexington, IN

Published by

Deer Trail Publishing

8681 W. New Bethel Road
Lexington, Indiana 47138
812-866-5504

Cover Design by: Dorothy Darnall Jones

Acknowledgements

The author is indebted to all who
helped make this book a reality.

Special thanks to everyone who allowed us to use their photos and art designs especially The Madison Courier and the Madison - Jefferson County Public Library.

To the many people who helped in so many ways. Their names are too numerous to mention, but to all of you...

THANK YOU !!!

Photographs

We wish to thank all of the photographers that contributed photos to this book, including: The Madison Courier, The Cincinnati Enquirer, The Indianapolis Star, The Louisville Courier-Journal, The Lexington Herald-Leader, and the Indiana Madison - Jefferson County Public Library.

THANK YOU !!!

All photos used by permission.

Many of the photographs in this book are reproduced from historical archives and therefore, the quality varies widely throughout. We have reproduced all the photographs, using the latest techniques, in order to match the original photographs as closely as possible.

Dedication

This book is dedicated to my family.

Burke, Marci, and Corey Jones,
and to the memory of my husband Marsh H. Jones, Jr.

Thank you for all of the support and assistance
in making this book become a reality.

Table of Contents

EMILIE PARIET TODD HELM

INTRODUCTION

This is a true story of a woman in the nineteenth and twentieth centuries, her background, her family, her education, the Civil War divisiveness and devastation, and her life as a single mother and widow for sixty-seven years!

Christmas time in 2005 it was my pleasure to volunteer as a docent in homes on the Christmas tour in Madison, Indiana, which is sponsored by the Madison Visitor's Center. My second assignment was in the home of Glen and Lisa Spencer, and their children Grace, Nathan, Olivia, and Ava, at 610 West Main Street. I had toured the garden and first floor previously when it was owned by another family. The house is known in Madison as the Emilie Todd Helm house—Emilie being the half sister of Mary Todd Lincoln, wife of President Abraham Lincoln. As an Episcopalian, I had always heard that Emilie Todd Helm on her first visit to Christ Episcopal Church at Third and Mulberry Streets had picked up her very own Book of Common Prayer in the pew rack. Union troops ransacked homes in the south and perhaps someone found her book and left it at Christ Episcopal Church. Furthermore it was said that Emilie Todd Helm was the organist at Christ Episcopal Church. In the 1960's and 1970's, in our summer residence on our houseboat in Madison, I recall reading tourist brochures of Madison describing 610 West Main Street as the residence of Emilie Todd Helm, widow of Brigadier General Benjamin Hardin Helm, Confederate States of America, and half sister of Mary Todd Lincoln, wife of President Abraham Lincoln.

As I perched on my stool in the kitchen, guests asked—this is a big house, did Mrs. Helm have any children? I smiled, and replied that I did not know, but I would find out. Another guest asked who Emilie and Mary's parents were, that she knew they had the same parents. I knew enough to answer that they were half sisters, obviously with the same surname they had the same father, but different mothers. I assured the guest that since I live across the street from the library I would delve into the Todd family relationships. My intellectual curiosity was stimulated! All I knew was that the house in Historic Madison was Greek Revival and built around 1850 and its rating was contributing or C in the Jefferson County Interim Report. The house faces west looking at the very large natural brick mansion of the Weber family. The Union Brewery, owned by Peter Weber, was just east of the Emilie Todd Helm house and that building was completely destroyed by fire in 1939. What were facts in the statements regarding Emilie Todd Helm, and what was fiction? What myths were perpetuated by Madison's story tellers? I have always enjoyed a love of history—and thus began my search to get better acquainted with Emilie Pariet Todd Helm!

THE TODD FAMILY GENEALOGY

And so the story begins!

Research started in the local history room of the Madison Jefferson County Public Library. In City Directories I found Emilie T. Helm was a resident of Madison 1866-1874 and resided first at 116 Presbyterian Avenue on the north side between West and Poplar Streets which is now a part of King's Daughters Hospital, and then at 610 West Main Street! Later I discovered that Mrs. Elizabeth L. Todd (Emilie's Mother) also resided in the same places at the same times!

But first I realized I had to learn about the Todd family! The internet provided me with wonderful genealogy information which I supplemented with other resources. The Todd family was prominent in Kentucky. Robert Smith Todd—Emilie's father--and his family resided in Lexington, Kentucky. Robert Todd's father, Levi, was born in 1756 in Montgomery County, Pennsylvania, was educated in Virginia where he studied law and he became a surveyor. Levi Todd was an officer under George Rogers Clark and rose to the rank of Major General. As a pioneer of Kentucky where Levi settled in 1776, he lived at Fort Harrodsburg, Logan's Fort, and Todd's Station. He became one of the first lot owners in the newly found city of Lexington on December 2, 1781. He built a brick residence outside the city limits of Lexington on the Boonsboro Road and named it "Ellerslie" after the Todd ancestral home in Scotland.

Robert Smith Todd – Father of Emilie Todd Helm

Levi married Jane "Betsy" Briggs, daughter of Captain Samuel and Sarah (Logan) Briggs on February 25, 1779. From 1781 to 1799 they had eleven children—six girls and five boys. After the death of his first wife, Levi married Mrs. Jane Holmes-Tatum and they had one son—probably in 1807. Amazingly, all of Levi Todd's children lived to maturity! General Levi and Jane Todd's first child was Hannah, born in 1781 at Logan's Fort and was believed to have been the first white child born in Kentucky! Hannah later married the Reverend Robert Stuart, and their son, John Todd Stuart was a senior law partner and friend of Abraham Lincoln. Robert Smith Todd's brothers and sisters lived in Kentucky, Illinois, and Missouri.

Robert Smith Todd was the seventh child of General Levi and Jane Briggs Todd. He was born February 25, 1791 in Lexington, Kentucky. Robert Smith Todd was graduated from Transylvania University at age 18, and was admitted to the bar at age 20 after studying with George Bibb, a chief justice of the State Appeals Court and later a United States senator. Robert Smith Todd never praticed law. The War of 1812 changed his plans, and after the war there were too many lawyers in Fayette County, and Robert became a merchant, state politician, bank president, and textile manufacturer. Public service also was involved. Robert was appointed a trustee of Transylvania University in 1827, was an active Presbyterian, an officer of his Masonic lodge, a director of a fire company, a city magistrate, and a member of the Kentucky state legislature. (Baker 1987:12-13)

His first wife was Elizabeth (Eliza) Parker, born in 1794 and a distant relative of Robert Todd. Eliza was the daughter of Robert and Elizabeth Porter Parker. They married November 26, 1812, and Robert and Eliza had seven children.

Elizabeth P. Todd   Birth 18 Nov 1813 Lexington, Fayette, Kentucky
          Death 11 Feb 1888. Springfield, Illinois
          Spouse Ninian Wirt Edwards   Marriage 16 Feb 1832
                                        Lexington, Fayette, Co. Ky.

Frances Jane Todd   Birth 7 Mar 1815   Lexington, Fayette, Kentucky
          Death 14 Aug 1899 Springfield, Sangamon, Illinois
          Spouse Dr. William Wallace   Marriage May 1839
                                          Springfield, Sangamon, Il.

Levi Oldham Todd   Birth 25 June 1817   Lexington, Fayette, Kentucky
          Death 18 July 1864   Broadway Hotel, Lexington, Kentucky
          Spouse Louise Searles   Marriage 16 Jan 1843
          Separation

Mary Ann Todd   Birth 13 Dec 1818   Lexington, Fayette County, Kentucky
          Death 16 July 1882   Springfield, Sangamon, Illinois
          Burial 19 July 1882   Springfield, Illinois Oak Ridge Cemetery
          Spouse President Abraham Lincoln
          Marriage 4 Nov 1842 Springfield, Sangamon, Illinois

Robert Parker Todd   Birth ca May 1820   Lexington, Fayette, Kentucky
                        Death July 1822   Lexington, Fayette, Kentucky

Ann Marie Todd or   Birth ca 1824   Lexington, Fayette, Kentucky
Ann Maria Todd   Death 21 March 1891 California
                        Spouse Clark Moulton Smith
                        Marriage 26 Oct 1846 Springfield, Illinois

George Rogers Clark Todd Birth 2 July 1825 Lexington, Fayette, Kentucky
                        Death 1902   Barnwell, South Carolina
                        Occupation physician
                        Spouse Ann H. Curry Marriage 1854 Canada Divorce
                        Spouse Martha Belton Lyles   Marriage ca 1868
(McCreary 2005 Mary Lincoln/Todd Family Genealogy)
(Ruesink 2006 Family Group Sheet).

Eliza Parker Todd died in 1825, a few days after the birth of her seventh child, at age 31. (Baker 1987:22) Robert and Eliza Todd probably lived with Eliza's mother until they moved into their new house built on the lower half of Widow Parker's lot on Short Street in Lexington in 1814. After the death of Eliza, Robert Todd then married Elizabeth "Betsey" Humphreys on November 1, 1826 at the home of her mother, Mrs. Alexander Humphreys, in Frankfort, Kentucky. (Baker 1987:28) Elizabeth Humphreys was born in 1800. Robert Smith Todd's second wife, Elizabeth Humphreys Todd, was twenty-six years old at the time of their marriage. Elizabeth, or "Betsey", Humphreys was the sixth of seven children born to Dr. Alexander and Mary Brown Humphreys in Staunton, Virginia. Dr. Humphreys earned degrees in medicine and surgery at the University of Edinburgh. He settled in Staunton, Virginia in 1787. Dr. Humphreys was a trustee of Staunton Academy when it was created in December, 1792, and entered into partnership with Dr. George McIntosh to practice physic and surgery. Mrs. Humphreys moved to Frankfort, Kentucky, after Dr. Humphrey's death in 1802. She built a house on Second Street which was later known as Haggin House.

Elizabeth (Betsy) Humphreys Todd - Mother of Emilie Todd Helm

Robert and Elizabeth (Betsey) had nine children.

Robert Smith Todd or
Robert Humphreys Todd

Birth 1827 Lexington, Fayette Co., Kentucky
Death 1827

Margaret Todd

Birth 14 Dec 1828 Lexington, Fayette Co., Kentucky
Death 13 Mar 1904 Daytona Beach, Florida
Spouse Charles Harry Kellogg
        Lexington, Fayette Co., Kentucky
Marriage 28 Oct 1847

Samuel Briggs Todd or
Samuel Brown Todd

Birth 25 Mar 1830   Lexington, Fayette Co. Ky.
Death 7 Apr 1862   Mississippi
Spouse Clelie or Cletie Cecile Royer
Marriage 1856

David Humphreys Todd

Birth 20 March 1832 Lexington, Fayette Co. Kentucky
Death August 1871 Huntsville, Alabama
Spouse Susan Turner or Susan Turner Williamson
Marriage 4 April 1865 Marion, Alabama

Martha K. Todd

Birth 9 June 1833 Lexington, Fayette Co. Kentucky
Death 9 July, 1868 Anna, Illinois
Spouse Clement Billingslee White
Marriage 1852

Emilie/Emily Pariet Todd

Birth 11 Nov 1836 Lexington, Fayette Co. Kentucky
Death 20 Feb.1930. Helm Place, Lexington, Kentucky
Spouse Benjamin Hardin Helm
Marriage 20 March, 1856 Frankfort, Kentucky

Alexander H. B. Todd or
Alexander Humphreys Todd
(Aleck or Alex)

Birth Feb. 1839 Lexington, Fayette Co. Kentucky
Death 5 Aug 1862 Baton Rouge, Louisiana

Elodie Breck (Jane) Todd

Birth 1 April, 1840 Lexington, Fayette, Kentucky
Death 1877 Selma, Alabama
Spouse Nathanial Henry Rhodes Dawson
Marriage 15 May 1862

Katherine Bodley Todd
(Kitty)

Birth 7 October 1841 Lexington, Fayette Co. Kentucky
Death 17 April 1875. Louisville, Jefferson Co. Kentucky
Spouse William Wallace Herr
Marriage 11 Jan 1866

(McCreary 2005 Mary Lincoln/Todd Family Genealogy)
(Ruesink 2006 Family Group Sheet)

Eight of Robert and Betsey Todd's children lived to maturity which is very unusual in that era. Friends of Eliza and Robert Smith Todd, Henry and Lucretia Clay lost five of their six daughters, and within a single year, Richard and Margaret Anderson's four of eight children died during a cholera outbreak. Some parents were reluctant to have a close association with their babies as death so often occurred, and mothers often did not survive childbirth. (Baker 1987:19)

THE TWO COMBINED TODD FAMILIES

Betsey and Robert Todd House
578 W. Main Street
Lexington, Kentucky

Elizabeth Todd Edwards – Emilie Todd Helm's Oldest Half-Sister

Scholars report that Eliza Todd was an uncertain housekeeper, timid, and presumably a loving mother. (Baker 1987:29) Betsey was just the opposite! She had been a single woman and was independent, imposing rules on her new family unknown to them. Her mother's well trained domestic slaves were installed in the Robert Todd house at 511 West Short Street in Lexington, Kentucky. She continued to manage the Todd summer home, Buena Vista, near Frankfort, Kentucky, located south on U. S. 421. Both the Short Street house and the Frankfort summer residences have been demolished. Betsey and Robert Todd moved to 578 West Main Street in 1832. The fourteen room house was built in 1803-1806, and presumably provided more space for the family of eleven. The Todd children were well educated, regardless of their sex. It is reported that when Betsey's patience was tried by her four step-daughters, as it often was, Betsey would quote her mother's wisdom that it took seven generations to make a lady—time, she stated emphatically, that her disobedient stepdaughters did not have! (Baker 1987:29) Fortunately for the stepdaughters their maternal grandmother lived next door to them until they moved in 1832, and they frequently escaped the wrath and indignation of their stern stepmother by going to their grandmother's. Marriage also was an escape for the daughters of Eliza and Robert Smith Todd. In 1832 daughter Elizabeth married a Transylvania University law graduate--Ninian Wirt Edwards of Springfield, Illinois. (Baker 1987:48) Elizabeth's sisters, Frances, Mary, and Ann Marie, followed Elizabeth to Springfield on receiving her invitation. Frances married Dr.William S.Wallace in 1839. Mary visited Elizabeth and Frances the first time in 1836 after she finished Madame Mentelle's school. (Helm 1928:58)

The departure of Robert Smith Todd's third daughter somewhat embarrassed the girls' father who wished for peace and quiet in his domestic circle instead of the tumultuous quarrels between his second wife and his daughters. The arrival of Emilie Todd in 1836 increased the number of Todd children living at home to nine (Robert Humphreys Todd was deceased), and soon Betsey was pregnant again. The daughters left to avoid the tension of living under the same roof with their stepmother. Mary moved permanently to Springfield in 1839. (Baker 1987:79) Ann Marie moved to Springfield, presumably sometime after Frances Todd's marriage. Ann married Clark Moulton Smith in 1846. George Rogers Clark Todd, Eliza and Robert Smith Todd's youngest child, testified under oath that Betsey had tried "to poison" his father's mind against the first Todds and that his stepmother's "relentless persecutions" had forced their first children "to abandon" their father's house. This statement was made by a Todd child who had been reared by Betsey from infancy! (Baker 1987:75)

The daughters were not the only ones to leave the Todd domicile. The sons were somewhat dysfunctional! The oldest of Robert Todd's sons, Levi Oldham, was described as an alcoholic, and at the time of his death in 1864 was separated from his family and living at the Broadway Hotel in Lexington. Betsey Humphreys Todd buried Levi in an unmarked grave in the family cemetery lot in Lexington. (Baker 1987:223) George Rogers Clark Todd left home in October, 1846, the same month as Ann's marriage, to live at the Megowan Hotel when he was a medical student at Transylvania University. George was described as erratic. (Baker 1987:329) Two of Betsey Humphreys Todd's sons, Samuel and David, went to New Orleans to be associated with Betsey's brother,

14

James Humphreys, on his prosperous sugar plantation. David Humphreys Todd at age fourteen ran away from home to look for silver and gold in California. His family was aghast when David returned home with a Chilean flag tattooed on his arm! (Baker 1987:223) Alexander Todd was in Muhlenberg County, Kentucky, managing the land of his uncle, David C. Humphreys in1860. (McMurtry 1943:31-32) Perhaps some of the dysfunctions were the result of Robert Smith Todd's absence from home thirty percent of the time due to business responsibilities. Other changes can be explained by the death of Robert Smith Todd in 1849 in a cholera epidemic. (Baker 1987:33-34)

Robert Todd had one slave for every white member of his family in 1830, when there were ten family members. The slaves cleaned the house and stables, washed, laundered, and sewed the clothes; cooked the meals; tended the children and horses, and purchased the food for ten Todd's. (Baker 1987:62) In Lexington half of the city's families depended on slave labor.

EMILIE'S EARLY YEARS

Emilie Pariet Todd was born November 11, 1836, in Lexington, Kentucky. Emilie was named for Emilie Parret Humphreys, the wife of Emilie Todd's Uncle Alexander Humphreys. Emilie was the sixth child of Robert and Betsey Todd. She had a splendid education by Harriet Stanwood in Lexington, Stuart Robinson, the Presbyterian minister of Louisville, and the Cincinnati Conservatory of Music. Harriet Stanwood later became the wife of James G. Blaine, who was Secretary of State under President James Garfield. (Confederate Veteran Vol. IV 1896:289-291)

Mary Todd Lincoln
Half-sister of Emilie Todd Helm
Wife of Abraham Lincoln

Abraham Lincoln
Husband of Mary Todd Lincoln
President of the United States

Mary and Abraham Lincoln were married by Dr. Charles Dresser, an Episcopal minister, in Elizabeth and Ninian Edward's home in Springfield, Illinois on November 4, 1842. (Baker 1987:97-98) Robert Todd Lincoln and Edward Baker Lincoln had blessed their marriage, and Mary was homesick and wanted her Kentucky relatives to meet their two sons. Abraham Lincoln, now a member of Congress in 1847, took Mary home to see her family before the Lincolns were established in Washington for the winter.

This was Mary's first visit home since their marriage. Mary's younger brothers and sisters had never seen her, and the entire family welcomed them warmly. The slaves filled the rear of the hall to shake hands with Mary and meet her husband and admire her children. Their timing was profound, as Mary's father died in a cholera epidemic July 16, 1849. Sam Todd returned home from Centre College and loved being called Uncle Sam by Robert Lincoln. When Abraham Lincoln met Emilie he remarked "So this is Little Sister," and thereafter Lincoln always called Emilie "Little Sister." (Helm 1928:99-100)

Emilie Todd – Abraham Lincoln's "Little Sister"

The Todd families' life changed drastically in 1849 with the death of Robert Smith Todd in a cholera epidemic at age 58. (Baker 1987:125) His will had only one witness signature instead of the required Kentucky two witnesses. Even lawyers make mistakes. The Todd house at 578 West Main Street had to be sold and the 1850 Franklin County, Kentucky, census has Betsey Todd living in District 1 with seven children at home. Betsey and her children obviously moved to Buena Vista, their summer home near Frankfort when Robert Smith Todd died in 1849. An inventory of the estate of R. S. Todd of his farm in Franklin County, Kentucky, and his house in Lexington was taken September 20, 1849. A sale of his personal property ensued on September 28, 1849. David C. Humphreys, Betsey Todd's brother from Versailles, Kentucky, purchased over $2,000 of R. S. Todd's property, and Betsey Todd purchased a carriage for $200.

Mary Todd Lincoln returned to Kentucky in the summer of 1851 and visited her step-mother at Buena Vista near Frankfort, Kentucky. (Helm 1928:102) She had with her Robert and Willie, Edward having died in February, 1850. Emilie Todd was fourteen years old and was fascinated by the reminiscences of Mary and Betsey Todd as they exchanged family news. They also talked of politics and the large issues of the day. Mary was also kind and courteous to the old slaves who happily reminded her of her childhood pranks she played at their expense. Emilie anxiously waited to visit her four sisters in Springfield—she was totally impressed with Mary's vivacious personality. Emilie's visit to Springfield occurred when she was about eighteen in 1854.

BEN HARDIN HELM

Mr. & Mrs. Ben Hardin Helm

Emilie met Benjamin Hardin Helm while Ben Helm was serving in the General Assembly of the Kentucky State Legislature. Emilie and Ben were married in Frankfort on March 20, 1856, with a reception at Buena Vista. This union would last even beyond his death.

John LaRue Helm

Ben Hardin Helm was the oldest child of John LaRue and Lucinda Barbour Hardin Helm, and was born in Bardstown, Kentucky June 2, 1831. Eleven of the twelve children born to Lucinda and John Helm lived to maturity. Ben Helm's father was Governor of Kentucky 1850-1851, and again in 1867. (McMurtry 1943:3) John Helm also served in the Kentucky House of Representatives, and was speaker of the House. John Helm helped create the Louisville-Nashville turnpike, and was on the Louisville Nashville Railroad Company Board of Directors and was also President of the Railroad Company. Lucinda and John Helm were from well-known, affluent families and John Helm was very successful. At one time John Helm owned more than forty slaves. (http://www.aths.com/johnLaRueHelm.html)

Helm Place – Elizabethtown, Kentucky

During the war, Union soldiers stationed in Elizabethtown devastated Helm Place and land, and encouraged their slaves to abandon the Helms. By the end of the war John Helm had to borrow money so the family could survive.

Benjamin Hardin Helm – Cadet, United States Military Academy, West Point, New York

19

Ben Helm was graduated from the Elizabethtown Seminary when he was just 15 years old. He was too young to attend West Point, so he attended the Elizabethtown Military Academy for one year and entered West Point on July 1, 1847. Benjamin Hardin Helm graduated ninth in a class of forty-two in 1851. (McMurtry 1943:5-7) There were nine graduates in his class who received the rank of general—six were Union officers and three were Confederate officers. Ben Hardin Helm's name was the best known name of all of them. He was given command of a cavalry unit and sent to Texas, but became ill with inflammatory rheumatism. On the advice of his father Ben resigned his commission on October 9, 1852, and entered the University of Louisville School of Law where he graduated in 1853. After the University of Louisville, Ben took a six month advanced law course at Harvard, and then entered into law practice with his father. Later he formed a partnership with his cousin, Col. Martin Hardin Cofer, with whom he was associated for some time in Elizabethtown. Benjamin was elected to the Kentucky House of Representatives in 1855. (McMurtry 1943: 7-10)

Ben Hardin Helm in 1857 went to Springfield, Illinois to argue a law case, and he called on the Lincolns with many messages from "Little Sister." The Lincolns gave him a double welcome as a Kentuckian and as a brother. The Lincolns insisted Ben stay with them and a friendship was formed. (McMurtry 1943:12-13) In the 1860 census Emilie and Ben Hardin Helm were listed as living in the sixth ward of Louisville, Kentucky, with two children and an Irish servant. Katherine Helm was born September 2, 1857, Elodie Helm was born March 7, 1859, and Benjamin Hardin Helm was born after that census, May 16, 1862.

In April, 1861 President Lincoln extended an invitation to the White House to Ben Hardin Helm in a personal letter. (Helm 1928: 182) Lincoln knew that Helm was a strong Southern-rights Democrat when he handed him a sealed envelope on April 27. The envelope contained a commission as paymaster in the United States Army with the rank of major. The rank of major at his age, thirty, was very exceptional in the army, and the position as paymaster was one of the most coveted in the service. Helm asked for a few days to consider the offer and that the offer not be made public.

Ben Helm longed to get back into the military service and this was a brilliant opportunity. He saw many of his old comrades and that same afternoon had a talk with Colonel Robert E. Lee of the Second Cavalry. Colonel Lee had just resigned his commission in the United States Army. Colonel Lee did not know that President Lincoln was Ben Helm's brother-in-law. Lee expressed the opinion that he could not strike at his own people, and that there must be a great war. Lee's advice to Helm was to do what his conscience and honor bid. (Helm 1928:185) Ben Helm was very flattered and gratified by the affection of the Lincolns and their estimate of his ability. The Lincolns told him goodbye and Ben Helm never saw them again. Ben Helm returned to Kentucky and met General Simon Bolivar Buckner, who had been his instructor at West Point, and his friend, Tom Monroe, then Secretary of State of Kentucky, and an impassioned States' Rights man. After consulting friends he wrote to President Lincoln declining the position of paymaster. (Helm 1928:187) Twice, in 1861 and 1862, Ben Helm thought of his would be benefactor, Abraham Lincoln, and sent the President kindly messages. (Confederate Veteran Vol. IV 1896:73)

AN OFFICER'S WIFE IN WAR TIME

Col. Ben Hardin Helm recruited the 1st Regiment of Kentucky Cavalry and presented it to General Albert Sydney Johnston on October 19, 1861. Col. Helm's first assignment was to occupy Bowling Green, Kentucky, with Brigadier General Simon Bolivar Buckner.

Todd Family Lot – Lexington Cemetery – Lexington, Kentucky

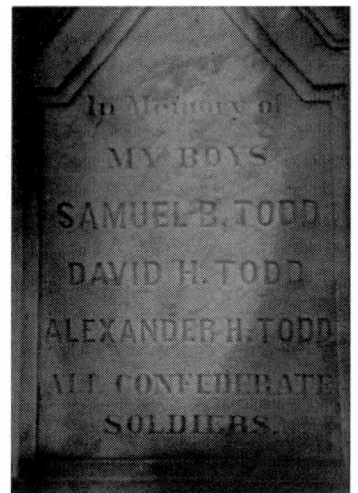

Todd Family Lot – Lexington Cemetery – Samuel, David & Alexander Todd

Alexander H. Todd   David Todd

Brothers of Emilie Todd Helm

Emilie's brothers were also in the Confederate army. Captain Samuel Briggs Todd enlisted in Company I, 24th Louisiana Regiment or "Crescent Regiment" of New Orleans, and was killed a month later leading a charge on the second day of the Battle of Shiloh with a sharpshooter's bullet through his temple on April 7, 1862. Alexander Todd was a Lieutenant and an aide-de-camp to Brig. Gen. Ben Hardin Helm. Alex Todd was killed by friendly fire at Baton Rouge August 5, 1862. (McMurtry 1943:33) David Humphreys Todd was a Captain in the Confederate Army, and for a time was in charge of Libby Prison in Richmond, Virginia, where according to some reports he tortured Yankee prisoners. (Baker 1987:223) David Todd was wounded at Vicksburg in July, 1863, and suffered from his wounds at Vicksburg until he died in Huntsville, Alabama, in August of 1871. Martha Todd's husband was Capt. Clement B. White in the Confederate Army, and Elodie Todd's husband was Col. N.H.R. Dawson in the Confederate Army.

Elodie Todd Dawson – Sister of Emilie Todd Helm

23

Margaret Todd Kellog – Sister of Emilie Todd Helm

Emilie's sister, Margaret, married Charles H. Kellogg in 1846. They spent a few years in New Orleans, and then lived in Cincinnati, Ohio. They were guests of President and Mrs. Lincoln in the White House when the first shot rang out at Fort Sumter in April of 1861. Charles Kellogg sought a patronage job from Lincoln, as did many of Mary Lincoln's Todd relatives by blood and marriage. Lincoln could not oblige Kellogg with a foreign appointment because of his pro-Southern political opinions. Kellogg claimed that any previous sympathies for the Southern cause ceased after the bombardment of Fort Sumter. Lincoln eventually appointed Kellogg a captain and commissary of subsistence on February 19, 1863.

Kellogg lied and never lost his Southern sympathies. Kellogg is accused of secret treason by Mark E. Neely, Jr. in his book IN THE SECRET TREASON OF ABRAHAM LINCOLN'S BROTHER-IN-LAW. In late winter of 1862 Kellogg made a trip into the Confederacy on business, and traveled with Emilie Helm's husband, General Helm. Kellogg aided his Louisiana Todd relatives by helping in the hospital for Louisiana regiments.

Despite his service to the cause, Kellogg was still a Yankee traveling in the Confederacy and thus aroused suspicion. Sometime in April of 1862 he was arrested by military authorities and placed in a prison in Montgomery, Alabama. Kellogg wrote Judah P. Benjamin, Confederate Secretary of War, and was transferred to prison in Richmond, Virginia where he was interrogated. Kellogg claimed he had come to the Confederacy to look after his mother-in-law, and the interrogator believed him and he was paroled to the city of Richmond. The letter to Benjamin and subsequent investigations did not reveal what Kellogg's mission was in the South or how he finally managed to return to Cincinnati. (http://www.historycooperative.org/journals/jala/17.1/neely.html)

Emilie's Springfield half-sisters and their husbands were all loyal to the Union. They were family as well as friends of the President of the United States and the First Lady, Abraham and Mary Lincoln. Emilie's half sisters, Elizabeth, Frances, Mary, and Ann Marie had all married Springfield men and had lived in Springfield since the1830's and 1840's. Levi Oldham Todd was a Union advocate, but his health was infirm, and he died in 1864 before the war was over. Emilie's other half-brother George Rogers Clark Todd was a Surgeon in the Confederate Army and in charge of Rickersville Hospital in Camden, South Carolina. (Baker 1987:222-223) George Rogers Clark Todd was the only child of Eliza and Robert Smith Todd who did not remain loyal to the Union. Perhaps his step-mother and half-brothers and sisters had a greater influence on him than he was willing to admit!

The Todd family was not the only distinguished Kentucky family that was divided. Border states naturally endured divided families in the conflict. Henry Clay, U. S. Senator and diplomat, had tried for many years to soothe the sectional strife that led to the war. Clay had three grandsons fighting for the Union and four serving the cause of the Confederacy. Kentucky U.S. Senator John J. Crittenden had two sons serving as general officers during the war: Major General Thomas L. Crittenden with the Union and his brother Major General George B. Crittenden for the Confederacy. (Soldier's Life, http://civilwar.bluegrass.net/SoldiersLife/brothervsbrother.html)

In February 1862, Colonel Helm had command of the 1st Kentucky cavalry and it had the duty to cover the retreat of General Albert Sydney Johnston from Bowling Green after the surrender of Fort Donelson and the evacuation of Nashville. Emilie Todd Helm was in Nashville at the time. Mrs. Helm asked a friend, Chauncey Brooks of Louisville, a brother-in-law of the Rev. Stuart Robinson, to drive her out to her husband's camp. Colonel Helm had broken camp and Emilie and Chauncey returned to Nashville. Mr. Brooks found a special car of the Vice-President of the Louisville and Nashville railroad for Mrs. Helm and her family to board. There was no room for her baggage except for one trunk which was put on top of an old fashioned carriage for $10. Colonel Helm came to the train in haste to tell Emilie he had made arrangements for them to go to Murfreesboro in a carriage, but they decided she should go by train to Chattanooga. Mrs. Helm and her children and servant boarded the last train out of Nashville for Chattanooga, Tennessee. Mr. Brooks continued to assist Emilie and her family en route to Chattanooga.

Emilie secured a room in the only hotel in Chattanooga. The weather was cold and they needed to prepare for some thousand to twelve hundred sick and convalescent soldiers from the hospitals at Nashville. They procured three large buildings and a force of Negro men and women were put to work cleaning them. Two bakeries were contracted with for bread, coffee, sugar and other supplies. Carpenters were set to work making cot frames and every bale of brown cotton cloth in Chattanooga was purchased to sew bed sacks for the cots of the wounded soldiers. The daughter and daughter-in-law of General Albert Sydney Johnston, Henrietta Johnston and Mrs. William Preston Johnston, willingly lent helping hands. While cutting cotton fabric for the bed sacks Emilie became faint due to the heat of the stove in the small room and poor food she had eaten. In fact, this writer determined that Emilie was expecting the birth of their third child in May 1862. Mr. Brooks found a bottle of Hostetter's Bitters which he gave Emilie without water. Emilie reported it would have resuscitated the dead. Emilie with brass thimbles and needles and thread and cotton sacks on her arm, recruited refugees to help sew the cotton sacks, and thus a great deal was accomplished. The sacks were filled with clean, fresh hay. (Confederate Veteran Vol. IV 1896:289-290)

Ben Hardin Helm
Confederate General

On April 6, 1862, at the end of the first day of fighting at Shiloh, Brigadier General Helm incorrectly sent word from his position in northern Alabama that Union Major General Don Carlos Buell's forces were pressing for Decatur, Alabama, instead of moving to Brigadier General U. S. Grant's aid. General Beauregard disregarded the message. Despite the flawed intelligence, General Beauregard announced Ben Helm's promotion to Brigadier General on April 17, 1862, effective March 14, 1862. (McMurtry 1943:30) A detailed account of Col. Helm's scouting activities at the time of the battle of Shiloh has never been revealed due to the secret nature of his work. His efforts won him praise by his superior officers. At Shiloh, Emilie Todd Helm's brother Captain Samuel Todd was killed April 7, 1862. (Helm 1928:201-202)

General Helm was sent to work on the defense of Vicksburg, Mississippi, in the summer of 1862. General Helm missed the Battle of Baton Rouge because of injuries sustained when his horse reared and fell on him. (McMurtry 1943:32-33) At Baton Rouge, Lieutenant Alexander Todd was killed by friendly fire on August 5, 1862. After the death of General Hanson at Stone's River, Gen. Helm was ordered to take command of the 1ˢᵗ Kentucky Brigade in January 1863. Brigadier General Helm was nicknamed "the gentle general." Ed Porter Thompson of the 6ᵗʰ Kentucky Infantry Regiment stated that they "loved him like a brother."

Ben Hardin Helm
Confederate General
Vicksburg 1863

In June of 1863 Gen. Helm served in the Mississippi campaign near Jackson, Mississippi under General Joseph E. Johnston to relieve General John C. Pemberton then under siege at Vicksburg. A bronze bust of Brigadier General Ben Hardin Helm was erected in the Vicksburg Military Park in 1914 on the South Loop, Kentucky Avenue, between Union and Confederate Avenues. Emilie's brother, Captain David Todd, was severely wounded at Vicksburg. After the fall of Vicksburg, General Joseph E. Johnston's army retreated over a pontoon bridge on the Pearl River at Morton, Mississippi, and rested a month. (McMurtry 1943:40-41) General Helm was sent by rail and steamer to Chattanooga to reinforce General Bragg.

In September, 1863, a fierce and ugly battle was fought at Chickamauga, Georgia. The Union Army, commanded by General William Rosecrans, and the Confederate Army, led by General Braxton Bragg, were approximately evenly matched in manpower, an unusual circumstance in major Civil War Battles. Each army had approximately 65,000 men.

Battle of Chickamauga – September 1863

Chickamauga was called the bloodiest two days in American history. Casualties at Gettysburg were greater, but that battle went on for three days. The battle at Antietam was known as the single bloodiest day.

The heavily-wooded battlefield left little room for maneuvering, and the two-day battle seemed as if it would degenerate into a simple slugging match. On September 20, confusion in orders left a gaping hole in Rosecrans' right flank which General James Longstreet exploited with an assault of four divisions. Almost half of the Federal army was routed and hastily retreated towards Chattanooga along with General Rosecrans and most of his staff. A total Union disaster was averted by the stand of General George Thomas' corps on Snodgrass Hill which held the left wing together long enough to organize an orderly retreat. This earned Thomas the nickname of "The Rock of Chickamauga." It was a great Confederate victory, but a costly one. Although Federal losses had exceeded 16,000, the Southern army had lost more then 18,000 casualties, including General Helm. Bragg felt his troops were in no condition to implement a rapid pursuit of the retreating Federals, who were allowed to fall back into defensive positions in Chattanooga. Occupying the heights overlooking the city, Bragg confidently waited for the Federals to either leave or starve.

On the morning of September 20, 1863, General Helm approached the day's battle calmly, laughing and joking as he mounted his horse for the attack. Leading his brave Kentuckians forward, the General waved his sword toward the LaFayette Road in their front and cried out "THIS is the road to Kentucky!" Soon after, he was hit in the right side by a bullet from the 15th Kentucky Infantry unit. At first he refused to dismount, but soon weakened by loss of blood he allowed himself to be helped to the ground and was carried on a litter to the rear.

After examining the wound, the doctors reluctantly told Gen. Helm there was no hope as the bullet had passed through his liver. As the battle of Chickamauga raged on and his Kentuckians continued to fight, General Helm was suffering and silent, preparing himself for death. That evening he roused himself to ask the outcome of the fight. Upon being told that the day belonged to the Confederates, he whispered the single word, "Victory!" He died with the satisfaction that his men had fought bravely and their efforts had been rewarded by victory. (Sons of Confederate Veterans 1998).

Helm Monument – Battle of Chickamauga – September 1863

Helm's Brigade at Chickamauga suffered severe losses. Three men out of four were either wounded or killed. In the battle of Chickamauga there were four brigade commanders on each side killed or mortally wounded. Each has a monument in the shape of a pyramid of eight inch shells, rising to a height of twelve feet on a base of limestone quarried in the park (Confederate Veteran 1896:290)

Emilie Todd Helm was visiting her sister Elodie Todd Dawson in Selma, Alabama, and barely arrived in Atlanta in time for her husband's funeral at St. Paul's Episcopal Church. Interment followed in the Atlanta Cemetery with military honors. Mrs. Helm remained a week longer as a guest of Col. W. H. Dabney, in whose home the General's body had been prepared for burial. (McMurtry 1943:46) Word of General Helm's death did not reach his parents in Elizabethtown, Kentucky, for three more weeks.

A WAR WIDOW IN WAR TIME

Mrs. Ben Hardin Helm
(Emilie Todd Helm)

The First Kentucky Brigade became known as the Orphan Brigade in the post war era. It was a general situation faced by the Kentucky Confederates, as they were never able to return to the state as a unit during the war. Emilie was thereafter honored to be known as the Mother of the Orphan Brigade. (Confederate Veteran Vol. IV 1896:290) General Breckinridge wrote Mrs. Helm after his death and said, "He loved them and they loved him," speaking of the soldiers in the Orphan Brigade and General Helm.

Emilie Todd Helm never remarried. Emilie set about the task of raising her children, as her husband would have expected of her.

After a week in Atlanta, Emilie visited Kentucky friends in Madison, Georgia. Governor John Helm notified Emilie's mother October 11 of his son's death. Lincoln sent a telegram to Dr. L. Beecher Todd, the Postmaster of Lexington, granting Mrs. Todd a pass to bring her daughter and children north to Kentucky. (McMurtry 1943:50-51) Mrs. Todd returned to Lexington with grandchildren Elodie and Ben Hardin Helm.

When Emilie and her oldest daughter arrived at Fortress Monroe, some scholars report that Emilie refused to take the oath of allegiance to the United States. (Baker 1989:223) Lincoln assumed that Mrs. Helm would take an oath of allegiance and granted her an amnesty oath. No one would be allowed to land without taking an oath of allegiance. The Federal officer at Fortress Monroe at Hampton, Virginia, telegraphed the President for further instructions and received a reply:

"Send her to me, A. Lincoln." (Helm 1928:221)

Emilie Helm was warmly greeted by the President and her sister. They were all grief stricken. Emilie's husband had been killed at Chickamauga, Willie Lincoln had died, and two of Emilie and Mary's brothers had been killed in the Confederate service, and one brother was mortally wounded.

The first evening Emilie and Mary dined alone. They had each suffered greatly in the last three years, and Emilie was a pathetic figure with her sad face and trailing black crepe dress. They talked of immaterial things, old friends in Springfield and Lexington and avoided painful subjects of politics and war. Emilie toured the White House with Mary. The Lincolns wished to keep Emilie's visit a secret as many Northerners would not relish her presence in Washington.

One day Senator Ira Harris and General Daniel E. Sickles paid the Lincolns a call. Dan Sickles had lost his leg at the Battle of Gettysburg and was incensed that a Confederate would be living in the White House. Public affairs would not be avoided with Senator Harris and General Sickles and Emilie angrily assured them if she had twenty sons "they would all be fighting yours." (Baker 1987:224)

General Sickles approached Mr. Lincoln privately and informed him he should not have that rebel in his house. Lincoln was angered by General Sickles' dictatorial manner and informed him that he was usually in the habit of choosing his own guests, and that Mrs. Helm was in the house because she had been ordered there. (Helm 1928:231)

Tad Lincoln was four years older than Katherine Helm and was entertaining his cousin. In showing Katherine photographs Tad commented on the photograph of his father that 'This is the President.' Katherine emphatically shook her head and replied that 'Mr. Davis is President.' Tad shouted 'Hurrah for Abe Lincoln,' and Katherine gave a hearty 'Hurrah for Jeff Davis.' Mr. Lincoln was amused by this heated argument and seated both Tad and Katherine on his lap and said 'Well Tad, you know who is your President, and I am your cousin's Uncle Lincoln.' In this manner he pacified both belligerents! (Helm 1928:231-232)

After spending nearly a week at the White House, Mr. Lincoln handed Emilie a paper to safeguard her from molestation, except as to slaves. Mr. Lincoln told Little Sister that he never knew her to do a mean thing in her life, and assured her that he knew she would not embarrass him on her return trip to Kentucky. Nothing was said then or afterwards about taking an oath of allegiance. Mary and Abraham Lincoln treated Emilie with loving kindness and consideration and were both greatly affected by the misfortunes of the Todd family. Emilie stated that it was 'the fortune of war,' and that while her husband loved Mr. Lincoln for his generous offer to make him an officer in the Federal army, he had to follow his conscience and side with his own people. (Helm 1928:233) Emilie left for Lexington with an invitation to return with her children for a long visit at the Soldier's

Home the next summer, but Emilie realized it would not be possible, as in reality her presence was an embarrassment to others.

Emilie and Katherine, Elodie, and Ben lived in Lexington with Emilie's mother. Kentucky was under martial law, and conditions were very trying under the rule of General Stephen G. Burbridge. (McMurtry 1943:61) Less than a year after she returned to Lexington, a malicious rumor of treasonable acts by Emilie Helm against the government was passed on to Lincoln.

The President wrote General Burbridge the following letter after hearing the rumor:

Washington, August 8, 1864

Major-General Burbridge, Lexington, Ky.:

Last December Mrs. Emily T. Helm, half sister of Mrs. L., and widow of the rebel General Ben Hardin Helm, stopped here on her way from Georgia to Kentucky, and I gave her a paper, as I remember, to protect her against the mere fact of her being General Helm's widow. I hear a rumor today that you recently sought to arrest her, but was prevented by her presenting the paper from me. I do not intend to protect her against the consequences of disloyal words or acts, spoken or done by her since her return to Kentucky, and if the papers given her by me can be construed to give her protection for such words or acts, it is hereby revoked pro tanto. Deal with her for current conduct just as you would any other.

A. Lincoln (McMurtry 1943:62)

Only once did Emilie Helm have occasion to use Lincoln's protection paper and that was when she asked a Federal officer to keep his troops who had camped near her home from trespassing and taking her family's food as it was being cooked in the kitchen! In this manner General Burbridge learned of her protection paper. Emilie Helm was never arrested and never lost her sense of obligation to President Lincoln. Emilie's position in Lexington society kept her in the eyes of the public and some Federal officers might have been resentful of her Southern leanings. (McMurtry 1943:63)

Emilie Todd Helm and a friend, Mrs. Bernard Pratt, obtained passes to go to Richmond in March of 1865 to see about the sale of cotton that Emilie owned. The timing was poor as Richmond was about to fall, and Mrs. Helm and Mrs. Pratt were advised to leave immediately, which they did on the next flag of truce boat. By orders of General E. O. C. Ord, Captain Robert Lincoln was ordered to accompany the women from Fortress Monroe to nearby Petersburg. The women arrived in Washington March 25, and registered at the Metropolitan Hotel. By this time Lincoln had secured from General Grant an order of protection of the cotton, the bulk of which was stored in Atlanta, Georgia, and had survived the scorched earth policy of the Confederates and the invading Federal armies. Before Emilie could sell the cotton or have it insured, the cotton was accidentally destroyed by fire. While in Washington and Baltimore on this business trip, the women did not call on the Lincolns, as they were visiting General Grant at City Point, Virginia at this time. (McMurtry 1943:67-68)

Another version of the sale of Emilie Helm's cotton is that she returned to Washington in the fall of 1864 demanding a license to sell 600 bales of cotton (Baker 1987:225) Lincoln had the power to grant such a permit, but he would not surrender his own code of honor while Emilie Helm remained a Confederate. Confederates were experiencing difficult economic times, and when Emilie returned to Lexington she wrote a letter to the Lincolns filled with frustration and anger. She was destitute and blamed the Lincolns for her emotional and economic sorrow. Emilie's letter created an unforgivable breach between the Lincolns and Emilie. This estrangement did not affect Emilie and her children's relationship with Robert Todd Lincoln, fortunately.

THE MADISON YEARS

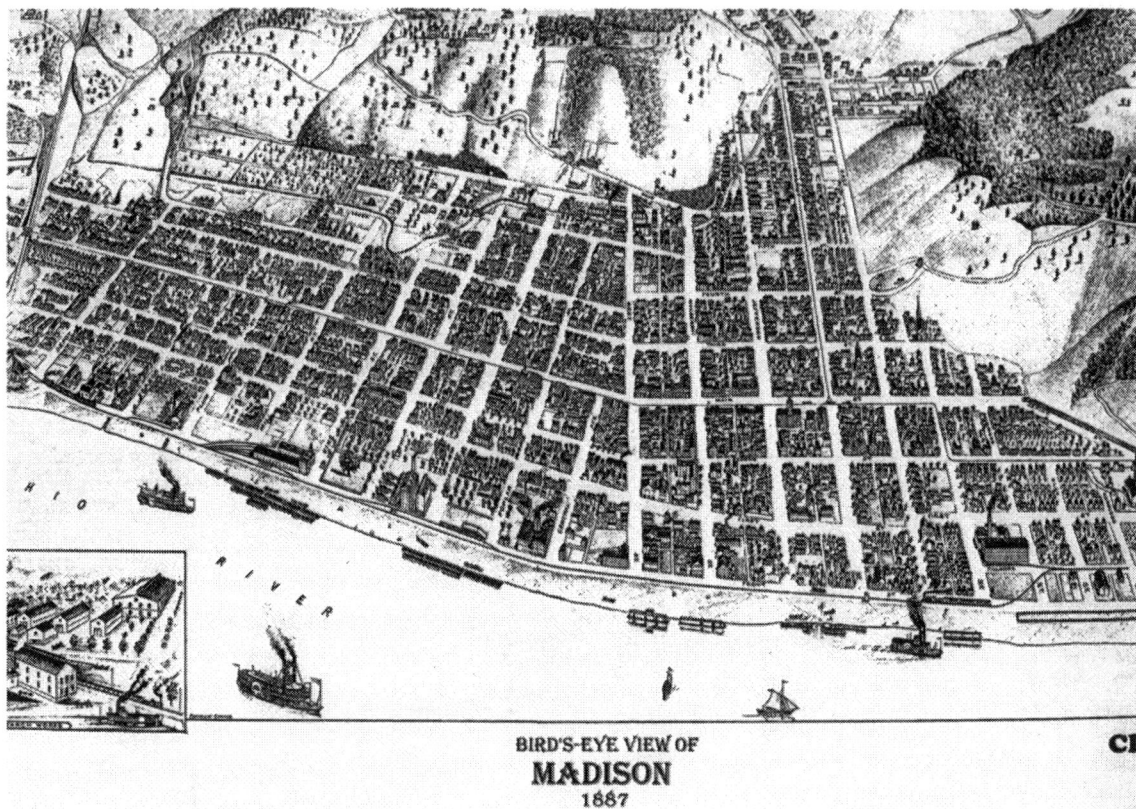

BIRD'S-EYE VIEW OF
MADISON
1887

Emilie Todd Helm, her Mother and three children moved to Madison, Indiana in 1866. Why did Mrs. Helm move to Madison? Perhaps Emilie moved to Madison because she felt she was a scapegoat. By virtue of her birth she was a half-sister of the former First Lady of the United States, Mary Todd Lincoln, and by virtue of choice Emilie was the widow of Brigadier General Benjamin Hardin Helm of the Confederacy. The harshness of living under martial law was certainly a factor. A search for close relatives has revealed only Todd second and third cousins living in Vernon and Vevay, Indiana. Madison had excellent access to steamboat and railroad transportation. Madison's political alignment was definitely with the Union, and Madison was prosperous compared to Lexington, Kentucky, and had educational opportunities for the children.

During the war years some businesses in Madison failed. A number of people moved from the community and the church struggled to survive. General John Hunt Morgan made his famous raid through Southern Indiana, and a military hospital was located at 1251 West Main Street in Madison. These were early post Civil War years, and a time of upheaval for the nation, the state, and the church.

Emilie Helm and her mother and three children came to the little city beneath the hills to establish a quiet rhythm of normalcy in their lives. They had survived the chaos of constant moves to be near General Helm. Emilie and her family survived the near poverty of war in the Confederate states and the deaths of General Helm, Captain Samuel Todd, Lieutenant Alexander Todd and the mortal wounding of Captain David Todd.

Madison offered the opportunity to bring order out of chaos, to enjoy the quiet beauty rather than the hectic, horrifying and terrifying war and martial law which they had endured. Madison was the new beginning of normal routines of family stability and progress in a small city that offered security, education and cultural opportunities.

Emilie Helm maintained her privacy in Madison after living a life as a member of prominent families in Lexington and Elizabethtown, Kentucky. No mention of Emilie is made in the social sections in Madison newspapers. Emilie and her children as a family lived longer in Madison, Indiana than any place other than their beloved Kentucky. The quiet beauty of the river and the hills and the view of Kentucky across the river must have been appealing and consoling to them.

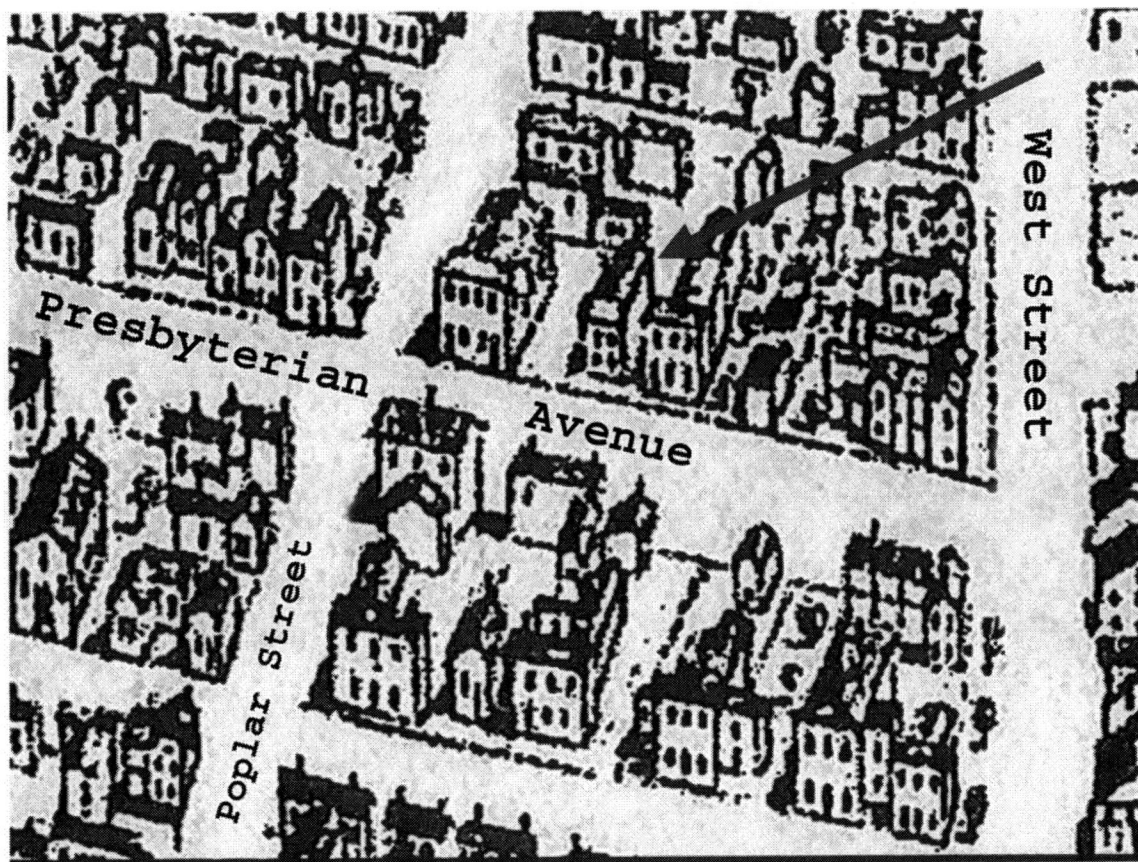

In February, 1866, Emilie Helm purchased a home at 116 Presbyterian Avenue between West and Poplar Streets. King's Daughter's Hospital is now located there. Emilie sold the property in May of 1871 and no notary was used. Instead Emilie went directly to the County Recorder, Joel Dickey, who wrote that she was "personally known to me as the grantor herein." The family then rented a home at 610 West Main Street.

Emilie Todd Helm house
610 West Main Street
Madison, Indiana

Emilie became the organist in Christ Episcopal Church where as an accomplished musician she earned a livelihood. (McMurtry 1943:68) Richard Dickie, Christ Episcopal Church Historian, reports no mention of Emilie Helm in church vestry minutes.

1875

2006

Christ Episcopal Church
506 Mulberry Street
Madison, Indiana

Katherine Helm was nine years old on their arrival in Madison, Elodie was seven and Ben Hardin was four years old. Katherine attended Miss Lydia Rutledge's Episcopal School and Miss Mary McFetridge's School of Higher Education. (Madison Courier June 22, 1937) Katherine also received her first formal art instruction from local art tutors in Madison, including the later quite successful artist, William McKendree Snyder. (Townsend, William H. Lexington Sunday Herald-Leader, February 10, 1946) It may be assumed that Elodie had a similar education in Madison and Elodie attended Mr. Hagen's College in Elizabethtown. (Niles, Rena Lexington Herald No date) Elodie also was a student at the Cincinnati Academy of Music studying china painting and glass enameling. (Townsend, William H. Lexington Sunday Herald-Leader, February 10, 1946)

Ben Helm was educated at Madison, Louisville, and Elizabethtown. Ben received a law degree at Professor Chenault's private school in Louisville. (Lexington Herald May 29, 1946) Emilie Helm was continuing the Todd tradition of an excellent education for the children in the family irrespective of their sex. The children's mother and grandmother were devoted to them.

Betsey Humphreys Todd died in their home February 14, 1874. The funeral was in Emilie Helm's home at 610 West Main Street in Madison, Indiana, and the interment was in the Todd family lot in Lexington, Kentucky. (Madison Evening Courier February 14,1874) Her will was probated in Jefferson County, Indiana, April 18, 1874.(Book B 136) Emilie was Betsey's only daughter who was a widow, and Emilie was generously remembered.

Emilie completed a course in thorough base in the Madison Musical Academy on the corner of Second and West Streets on October 14, 1874. Principal William E. Bates cheerfully recommended Emilie as entirely competent to teach that branch of music. Thorough base is a system of musical shorthand which uses the melody line and numbers that correspond to the chords that should be present.

BACK TO KENTUCKY

Emilie Todd Helm house
218 West Poplar Street
Elizabethtown, Kentucky

Emilie and her children moved from Madison to Louisville, where Emilie taught music. They are listed in the 1880 census as living in Elizabethtown, Kentucky. Emilie and her family lived at 218 West Poplar Street in Elizabethtown, a house that was built around 1820.

Katherine Helm

Katherine Helm was an accomplished artist. She studied art for six years in New York City, and her portraits are outstanding. (Townsend, William H. Lexington Sunday Herald-Leader, February 10, 1946) She painted all of Kentucky's early governors and several portraits of Mary Todd Lincoln. Her book, MARY, WIFE OF LINCOLN, was published in 1928 and is an excellent biography.

Elodie Helm Lewis

Elodie married Waller Lewis, a Scott County, Kentucky, farmer and stock breeder. Mr. Lewis died in 1908, and Elodie returned to live with her Mother and Katherine. Elodie and Waller Lewis had no children.

As noted, Ben Helm studied law and held prominent positions with the Louisville and Nashville railroad, the Chicago and Alton railroad, and the Chicago Great Western railroad, as well as being Commissioner of the New Orleans Bureau of Freight and Transportation. He never married, and his object in life was to take care of his mother and sisters. He did all he could for them as long as he lived. (Murphy 1995:13)

Ben Hardin Helm, Jr.

Emilie received an appointment from President Chester Arthur as Postmistress in Elizabethtown in 1883, and Emilie served three terms as Postmistress, ending in 1895. (McMurtry 1943:69) It is reported that Robert Todd Lincoln was influential in getting the appointment for his Aunt Emilie.

Benjamin Hardin Helm
Brig Gen KY Orphan Brig
Confederate States Army
June 2 1831   Sep 20 1863

Helm Family Cemetery
Elizabethtown, Kentucky

In 1884 members of the Orphan Brigade moved General Helm's body from Atlanta and reburied it in the Helm family's cemetery in Elizabethtown, Kentucky. Benjamin Hardin Helm is remembered less for his Confederate service than for marrying Emilie Todd in 1856. After Emilie Todd and Benjamin Hardin Helm were married, Emilie as the half-sister of Mary Todd Lincoln brought her husband into President Lincoln's family circle. (http://www.findagrave.com/cgi-bin/fg.cgi?page=gr&GRid=8925)

The Emilie Todd Helm chapter of the Daughters of the Confederacy was established in Elizabethtown in 1897. (Confederate Veteran Vol. VI 1898:554) Emilie was President of the woman's organization. Emilie remained active in Confederate reunions in the Daughters of the Confederacy and the Orphan Brigade. Emilie was loyal to the memory of the Confederacy, and enjoyed being with others who shared her love and loyalty.

Emilie Todd Helm
"Mother of the Orphan Brigade"
Circa 1886

Emilie was very productive in genealogy research. Her letters pertaining to genealogy research were given to the Kentucky Historical Society. Emilie and Katherine Helm worked on genealogy from 1880 to 1900. Emilie and Katherine protected and often changed the ages of women in the family. Emilie's grandmother commented that a woman's age was a 'changeable number' and Emilie heeded her grandmother's advice on several occasions. Even in census records Emilie changed her daughter's ages. To further protect their age, Emilie listed family members by reporting all the male children in their order of birth and then the female children in their birth order. (McCreary 2005 Mary Lincoln/Todd Family Genealogy) In fact, the birth order of Ann Marie and Robert Parker Todd, children of Robert and Eliza Parker Todd) was incorrect and was placed in proper order by this writer. (McCreary 2005 Mary Lincoln /Todd Family Genealogy) Dr. William Ruesink, a genealogy scholar, reports that age inaccuracies in genealogy records was a common practice.

Emilie destroyed many of her diaries, but some letters do remain. Three letters written by Emilie were found in the archives of the Western Kentucky University library. Two were written to Emilie's second cousin, Ella Scott Green, in Grayson County, Kentucky in 1891 and 1894, and the third to Ella Green's widower, Lafayette Green in 1896. The signature in all three letters written by Emilie was E-M-I-L-Y Todd Helm or E-M-I-L-Y T. Helm. However, Emilie's name on her tombstone in the Lexington Cemetery is spelled E-M-I-L-I-E.

Emilie Todd Helm signatures from two original letters in the Manuscripts & Folklife Archives, Western Kentucky University, Bowling Green, Kentucky.

Letter from Elizabethtown dated Sept 21, 1891, sent to her second cousin Ella (Scott) Green:

Letter from Elizabethtown dated 15 March 1896, sent to Mr. Lafayette Green, husband of her deceased cousin Ella (Scott) Green:

Helm Place
2575 Bowman's Mill Road
Lexington, Kentucky

Ben Hardin Helm, Jr. always told Emilie that he would purchase a farm when he accumulated enough money. Ben achieved his goal and purchased Cedar Hall at 2575 Bowman's Mill Road in Lexington in 1912. They renamed the estate Helm Place. It is unknown when Cedar Hall-Helm Place was built by Col. Abraham Bowman on the site of Todd's Station. (Murphy 1995:3) Todd's Station was built in 1778 by Emilie's grandfather, General Levi Todd. Col. Abraham Bowman acquired Todd's Station after his service in the Revolutionary War, and through a military grant, received several thousand acres of land.

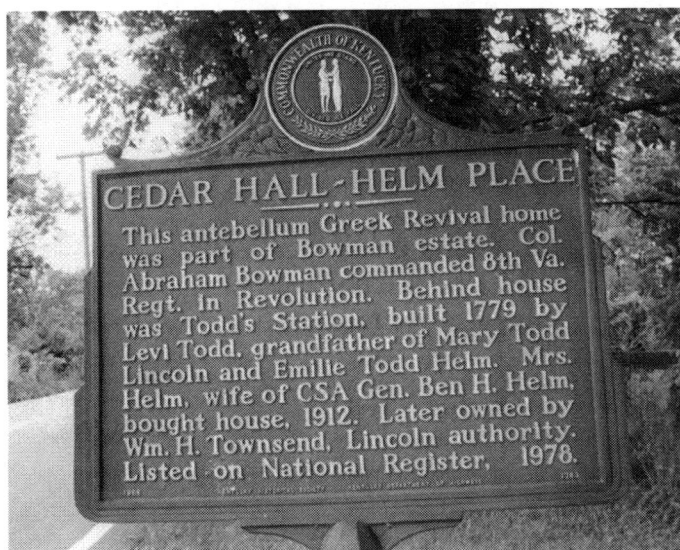

Note: Correction – Ben Hardin Helm, Jr. purchased the farm in 1912.

At Helm Place, Ben Hardin Helm, Jr. was engaged in burley tobacco farming. Mr. Helm objected to the regulation of tobacco growing legislated by President Franklin Delano Roosevelt's New Deal. He espoused the Republican Party of Uncle Abraham Lincoln, which his father, the illustrious general of the same name, opposed with his life! Ben Helm laughed as he told people it took a Roosevelt to make him a Republican. Ben Helm was a fierce individualist, and hated his individualism opposed by the New Deal. (Louisville Courier-Journal Magazine, February 11, 1940, page 4, columns 1-10). Niles, Rena Lexington- Herald No date}

Emilie and her children maintained a close relationship with Robert Todd and Mary Harlan Lincoln. Katherine Helm dedicated her book MARY, WIFE OF LINCOLN, to Mrs. Robert Todd Lincoln in 1928. Robert and Mary Harlan Lincoln commissioned Katherine Helm to paint a portrait of Mary Todd Lincoln On May 18, 1924, Mary Harlan Lincoln wrote to "Dear Aunt Emily, do you not think that we "Todds" ought to put our heads together and see to having a fine portrait of Robert's mother placed in the White House by the side of her husband? This is a project I have had near my heart for some time and I want dear Cousin Kate to paint it." Cousin Kate was of course delighted and in the next year and a half painted three portraits of Mary Todd Lincoln, one for the White House, one for Robert Todd Lincoln's own home in Washington, and one for the front parlor at Helm Place. (Murphy 1995:18-19) Katherine painted three more portraits of Mary Todd Lincoln for Dr. William E. Barton, Lincoln Memorial University, and Dr. William H. Townsend. (Townsend, William H. Lexington Sunday Herald- Leader, February 10, 1946)

On February 18, 1926, President and Mrs. Calvin Coolidge, in the presence of the artist, Katherine Helm, and a few close friends, in the Oval Room of the White House, accepted the gift of the portrait of Mrs. Lincoln from her son and daughter-in-law. The portrait hangs today in the Lincoln bedroom in the White House.

Robert and Mary Harlan Lincoln were generous financial supporters of Emilie and her children. They financed Katherine in the writing and publishing of her book. They also contributed other unsolicited monetary gifts to Emilie and her children. (Murphy 1995:19) Elodie and her companion, Elizabeth Brown, were en route to Robert and Mary Harlan Lincoln's estate, Hildene, near Manchester, Vermont when Elodie died in Geneva, New York in 1953. (Murphy 1995:32) Elodie and Miss Brown had planned to visit Mary [Peggy] Lincoln Beckwith, the granddaughter of Robert and Mary Harlan Lincoln.

Emilie and her children always had servants in their employ. At Helm Place they had a chauffeur, cook, and a jack of all trades. In all the censuses a servant was mentioned as a member of the household. (Murphy 1995:24)

Emilie Todd Helm
1896 – Age 60

Emilie Todd Helm was a beautiful, brilliant, and strong woman. Emilie stated that she bound her children together with love, reverence, and respect. (Lexington Herald February 20, 1930) She carried on responsibly as a single woman, and took care of her mother, saw to her children's education, and pursued various careers. Emilie was a survivor of a horrifically divisive and horrendously costly conflict. Emilie Todd Helm never remarried, but wore mourning for "the love of her life" as long as she lived—another sixty-seven years!

Emilie Todd Helm died at Helm Place February 20, 1930. (Lexington Herald February 20, 1930) Bishop H. P Almon Abbott of Christ Church Cathedral officiated at the funeral at Helm Place with the burial in the Todd lot in the Lexington cemetery. Katherine Helm died June 18, 1937, (Madison Courier June 22, 1937) Ben Hardin Helm died May 28, 1946, (Lexington Herald May 29, 1946) and Elodie Helm Lewis died June 12, 1953. (Lexington Herald June 13, 1953)

May their souls rest in peace, and may light perpetual shine upon them!

EMILIE
DAUGHTER OF
R.S. & E.L. TODD
AND WIFE OF
GENL. BEN HARDIN HELM
BORN NOV. 11, 1836
DIED FEB. 20, 1930

Emilie Todd Helm

KATHERINE
DAUGHTER OF
GENL. BEN HARDIN HELM
AND
EMILIE TODD
BORN SEPT. 2, 1857
DIED JUNE 18, 1937

Katherine Helm

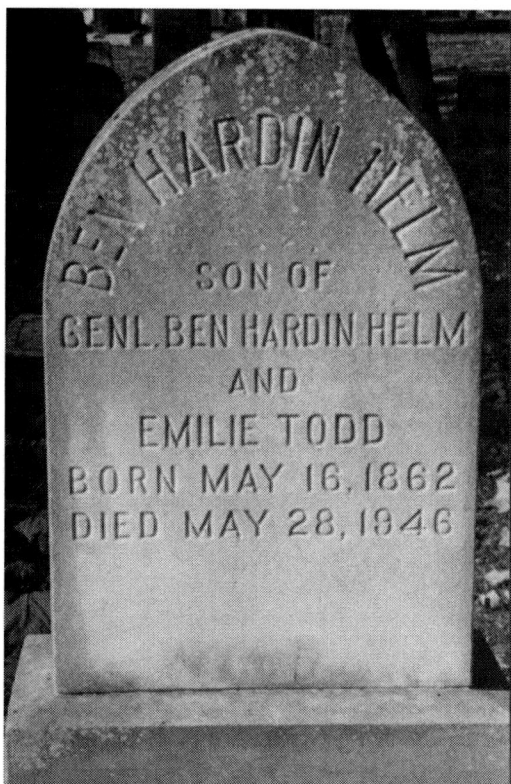

BEN HARDIN HELM
SON OF
GENL. BEN HARDIN HELM
AND
EMILIE TODD
BORN MAY 16, 1862
DIED MAY 28, 1946

Ben Hardin Helm

ELODIE
DAUGHTER OF
GENL. BEN HARDIN HELM
AND
EMILIE TODD
WIFE OF
WALLER H. LEWIS
BORN MARCH 7, 1859
DIED JUNE 12, 1953

Elodie Helm Lewis

APPENDIX

SOURCES

Baker, Jean H., Mary Todd Lincoln

Basler, Roy P., edited The Collective Works of Abraham Lincoln

Confederate Veteran

Fleishner, Jennifer, Mrs. Lincoln and Mrs. Keckly

Goodwin, Doris Kearns, Team of Rivals

Helm, Katherine Mary, Wife of Lincoln

Holzer, Harold, The Lincoln Mailbag

Jefferson County Interim Report, Indiana Historic Sites and Inventory

Madison Census

Madison City Directory

McCreary, Donna, Mary Lincoln/Todd Family Genealogy Information

McMurtry, R. Gerald, Ben Hardin Helm

Murphy, Mary Genevieve Townsend, The Story of Helm Place

Neely, Mark E. Jr. and R. Gerald McMurtry, The Insanity File: The Case of Mary Todd Lincoln

Randall, Ruth Painter Mary Lincoln, Biography of a Marriage

Ruesink, William E., Family Group Sheet

Lexington Herald
Lexington Leader
Madison Courier
Madison Evening Courier

Hardin County Public Library
Hardin County Historical Society
Jefferson County Historical Society Archives
Kentucky Historical Society
Lexington Library, Kentucky Room
Madison-Jefferson County Library, Local History Room

Janice Barnes
Kim Bland
Edward C. Darnall
Louis DeCar
Richard Dickie
Ron Grimes
Burke Jones
Corey Jones

Ken Knouf
Lynn Maricle
Sara Sanders
Dr. William Ruesink
Richard Skidmore
Heidi Valco
Robert Webb
Jerry Yarnetsky

REFERENCES CITED

Baker, Jean H.
    1987 Mary Todd Lincoln. W. W. Norton & Company, New York.

Confederate Veteran
    1896 Vol. III 1895. Vol. IV 1896. Vol. VI 1898.
    Broadfoot Publishing Co. Wilmington, N.C.

Helm, Katherine
    1928 Mary, Wife of Lincoln. Harper & Brothers, New York.

John LaRue Helm
    2006 http://www.aths.com/johnLaRueHelm.html

Lexington Herald
    February 20, 1930. May 29, 1946. June 13, 1953.

Madison Courier
    June 22, 1937.

Madison Evening Courier
    February 14, 1874.

McCreary, Donna
    2005 The Family of Mary Lincoln.
    http://members.aol.com/beaufait/biography/genalogy.htm

McMurtry, R. Gerald
    1943 Ben Hardin Helm. The Civil War Round Table, Chicago.

Neely, Mark E. Jr. 2005 The Secret Treason of Abraham Lincoln's
    Brother-in- Law
    http://www.historycooperative.org/journals/jala/17.1/neely.html

Murphy, Mary Genevieve Townsend
    1995 The Story of Helm Place. The Harrodsburg Herald, Harrodsburg,
    Kentucky.

Ruesink, Dr. William
     2006 Family Group Sheet
    Ancestry.Com,"Ancestry World Tree"(a subscription
    service),http://awt.ancestry.com/.

    Ancestry.Com, "Indiana Marriages to 1850" (a subscription service),
    http://search.ancestry.com/.

Ancestry.Com "One World Tree" (a subscription service},
http://trees.ancestry.com/.

Anonymous, "Benjamin Hardin Helm, General in the CSA Army", posted at Ancestor Chronicles – Our Kin And Their Times, http://groups.msn.com/AncestorChroniclesOurKinAndTheirTimes/civil war.msnw?action=get_message&mview=O&ID_Message=22164&Last Modified=4675481289405736152

Daughters of the American Revolution, Indiana, John Paul Chapter, Madison. 1945. "Items from early newspapers of Jefferson County, Indiana, 1817-1886", Madison-Jefferson County Public Library, Madison, Indiana.

Helm, Katherine, 1928. Mary, Wife of Lincoln, Harper &I Bros, New York & London.

Hoggatt, Ruth, "Jefferson County, Indiana, GenWeb site," http://www/myindianahome.net/gen/jeff/index.html.

Jefferson County Recorder's Office, Real Estate Records, Madison, Indiana

Kentucky Historical Marker Database, Cedar Hall-Helm Place (Marker Number: 1783), http://www.kentucky.gov/kyhs/hmdb/MarkerSearch.aspx?mode=Subject &subject=137.

Lindsey, Steven, "John LaRue Helm—Life and times of an Historic Kentuckian', http://www.aths.com/johnLaRueHelm.html

Madison City Directories, various years, Madison-Jefferson County Public Library, Madison, Indiana.

McCreary, Donna, "The Family of Mary Lincoln", http://members.aol.com/beaufait/biography/geneology.htm.

RootsWeb, "World Connect Project", http://worldconnect.rootsweb.com/. The Church of Jesus Christ of Latter-day Saints, Various on-line records, http://www.familysearch.org/

U. S. Federal Census for years 1850, 1860, 1870, 1880, 1900, 1910, 1920. Viewed at Ancestry.Com (a subscription service), http://search.ancestry.com/.

Soldier's Life Internet Brother vs. Brother
2006 http://civilwar.bluegrass.net/SoldiersLife/brothervssbrother.html

Sons of Confederate Veterans, Elizabethtown, Kentucky 1998
Internet
http://groups.msn.com/AncestorChroniclesOurKinAndTheirTimes/
civilwar.msnw?action=get_message&mview=1&ID_Message=221
64

Townsend, William H. Lexington Sunday Herald-Leader. February 10, 1946.